Welcome to Grandparenting

❧ Welcome to Grandparenting ❧

Rosemary Weis
Michelle Johnston

Welcome to Grandparenting
by Rosemary Weis & Michelle Johnston

Printed in the United States of America

ISBN 9781624197550

Unless otherwise indicated, Bible quotations are taken from the King James Version.

www.xulonpress.com

This book is in acknowledgement of the heroic efforts of grandmothers everywhere – past, present and future.

❧ *Dedications* ❧

This book is dedicated to my husband,
Mike Weis, the love of my life who makes all
things possible. A special thank you to Nana,
Josephine DiQuattro, my hero grandmother.
R.W.

This book is dedicated to my children,
Peter, Ryan and Laurel,
who give me more strength and courage
than they could ever know.
M.J.

❧ Table of Contents ❧

❧ ❧

Grandchildren are the crown
of the aged.

Proverbs 17:6

The New Oxford Annotated Bible
(RSV)

❧ ❧

❧ Welcome to Grandparenting ❧

$y$our prayers have been answered! Maybe you've just received the great news for the first time and you can't wait for the little bundle to arrive. Or maybe you're a grandparent many times over and are looking for new ways to enhance your grandparenting routine. Welcome to this book! Being a grandparent is a special opportunity life provides. We like to think of it as parenting once removed, but enhanced with the right to indulge and spoil children on a level which moms and dads can't hope to compete.

Our hope is that the advice and ideas we share greatly enrich the experience of grandparenting for you and your grandchildren. No matter how much or how little of this book you take to heart, always remember that you hold the power to make a child's life different. The memories you make together will last for generations!

We start this book at the beginning of the birthing experience, but feel free to thumb through to the chapters that apply to your situation if the grandchildren are here already.

Enjoy your blessings,

Grandma Rosemary & Mommy Michelle

❧ Section I ❧

You're Going to Be a Grandparent

❧ ❧

Whoever receives one little child like this in My name receives Me.

Mathew 18:5

❧ ❧

4

๛ Chapter 1 ๏

There's a Purpose to Grandparenting

$\mathcal{G}$randparenting truly is an instance where the journey is more important than reaching the end of the ride. Think about it. Do you really want to be the first to the finish line or do you want to stop and smell the flowers along the way? Grandparenting has its purpose and its historical place in the family for a reason. It's to benefit the newest generation. Through grandparenting you have another opportunity to create as many memories as possible and make a difference—not only in the lives of your grandchildren, but in the lives of your children as well.

By partnering with your children, you can help them raise their little ones the best possible way. The key to success is to remember to work as a team in the best interest of the children. Always respect the fact that the grandchild is their child first, and that mom and dad are the ones charged with making the final decisions (whether you agree with them or not). Much may have changed in the world, but the struggles of being a parent have not. You certainly can recall how hard parenting can be when you are trying to hold down a job, do chores and take care of the homestead. Your kids are just tired waking up in the morning! In your role as a grandparent, then, you should always strive to be part of the solution.

You may have a lot of ideas to help your kids raise the next generation, but we caution that before you do anything, clear it with the parents first (preferably out of earshot of the grandchildren). It works better for the child if everyone is pulling in the same direction. Recall that you are trying to enhance their parenting, not detract from it.

And, as much as possible, always ask your children, "What can I do to help you?" It is easy for the grandchildren to become the center of everyone's attention, especially in the case of first-time parents. Remember this is a period in their lives when your kids need the love and support of their own mom and dad too.

We worry about what a child will be tomorrow, yet we forget that he is someone today.

Stacia Tauscher

❧ Chapter 2 ❦

Generosity Takes Many Forms

*a*lmost everyone agrees to wishing for a little more – more money, more time, more resources, etc. The situation is different for everyone.

As you think about the strengths you can bring to grandparenting, consider what you have that you can comfortably share. For some, time may be a precious commodity, but money may not. For others, elbow grease may be in plentiful supply, but funds may not. And no matter what resources you have to freely share, distance to the grandchild could be a hampering factor.

It is important that you grandparent within your means, both in terms of time and money, otherwise the joy will be compromised. As you read the ideas in this book, challenge yourself to look for ways to deliver the same end result if you feel you don't have the time, talent or treasure we suggest drawing upon. Feel free to twist, substitute or re-imagine any idea you find appealing. There is always a way if you have the will. Your grandchildren and children most certainly will benefit from your efforts.

If you are uncertain as to how to help, pray on it. Spend time alone with God and ask for wisdom. An answer will come!

❧ Chapter 3 ❧

The Baby's On the Way

*W*hat to do for nine months? Believe it or not, this is a perfect time for planning for the future to reduce the workload later. Both parents and grandparents can do it, and you can lead the way.

Cook Once, Eat Twice. Make the most of freezer space. Help the new parents invest in a separate freezer if space allows, or simply help them organize the one above their refrigerator. If you live nearby, consider putting a portion of your own freezer space at the new parents' disposal. The goal is to lay in a supply of home cooked meals, soups, baked goods, and favorite foods in disposable cookware that will help the new parents through the first few weeks when baby is up at night and mom isn't back to fighting form. We do not recommend making casseroles in your good cookware that the new parents then have to clean and return to you. You are not looking to make work for them. Mom is going to be very tired, especially if she is nursing, and has enough to do already. (See Chapter 23 for ideas for freezer-friendly meals.)

House Chores. Help the parents shampoo the rugs, wash curtains, clean the gutters, refresh the landscaping, etc., long before the ninth month. A good spring cleaning inside and out will allow the new parents to coast for months after the baby arrives. You can make it a project for you and your child to complete together; or you can call in the troop of siblings, friends and neighbors who may also be looking for ways to lend a hand. If physical conditions prevent you from helping directly, you may want to make it an early present to pay for a one day spring cleaning or landscaping from a qualified professional service. Or, offer to pay for a teenage "mother's helper" for a week's time.

Car Service. Just like the house, the car might benefit from a little TLC prior to bringing baby home from the hospital. Encourage and assist the new parents in getting a thorough car inspection — from tire rotation and oil change to detailing and baby-proofing. This may be an especially helpful gift to a single mom.

Family Historian. Think to record elements of yourself and your family's history that new parents will not be thinking about in the haze of dirty diapers and sleepless nights. Take pictures that can be used in the baby's scrapbook, such as one of your current home so your grandchild will always remember "grandma's house." Since you may move through the years, write down your address and phone number too. Take pictures of great aunts, uncles and cousins, and be sure to label them. Fill in as far back as you can recall of the family tree. These photos and information will enable someone (perhaps you?) to put together a heritage album for the child someday, if these items are not used in the baby book itself.

Start a Birthday Time Capsule. Make a time capsule of the day/month the baby is born. Save not only the front pages of a local and national newspaper from the day the baby is born, but also a few general interest or news magazines. Place all of this in a plastic sleeve and hand it to the parents to put aside for baby. Just for fun, write down the cost of various grocery items, a gallon of gas, postage stamps, a movie ticket, etc., as of the baby's time of birth. You could also include sales flyers from local stores so that your grandchild can one day see styles and prices from "back when." You could choose to repeat this on the child's birthday every year or every few years to create a longer lasting record of change.

Sponsor Couple Time. This is a time when mom and dad need to spend time together as adults before their world turns upside down. If there are other children on the scene, offer to baby-sit now and then so that they can have some alone time. Or pay for a sitter for a night if you can afford it. Sharing discount cards or coupons for local restaurants and video stores is another budget-friendly option for encouraging quality time.

Pass Along Parenting Info. If you can do so without upsetting anyone's feelings, offer the new mom or dad some of the parenting books you thought valuable when navigating sleepless nights, teething and tantrums. Or, use the internet to dig up "old-fashioned" parenting advice so you can all share a laugh on how common wisdom has changed through the years. (How did we survive childhood without seat belts and car seats?) Another option is to send the parents a subscription to a parenting or family magazine that will have loads of advice and tips for them.

Clip Coupons. Who would have thought that such a small little bundle of joy could impact the budget so much! If the parents-to-be don't mind, clip and send them money-saving coupons for any and all of the baby items they will soon need. Diaper coupons will probably always be welcomed, but coupons for sippy cups, clothing, and items to baby-proof the home are also a possibility. If you are Internet savvy, look for online savings too. In addition to clipping coupons, you can also scout out free samples of baby items to pass along.

Nursery Time. Help the parents decorate the nursery if they are open to including you. An extra hand painting or assembling furniture is almost always welcomed. (If you physically cannot help with the work, offer to pay for the paint or furniture assembly service.) Once you know the theme, look for creative ways to enhance it. If you are crafty, embroider a blanket to match, paint a piece of furniture, or help make the drapes. If that's not your style, consider stocking the closet with baby hangers or decorating a plastic storage box with simple designs using permanent markers.

Bulk Purchasing. If you or the parents-to-be have a membership to a wholesale shopping club, take advantage of it for the terrific savings. While you may not know the sex or the name of the baby, you do know he or she will use diapers and wipes by the case! To spread out the costs, for each month of the pregnancy focus on a different area of the house that could benefit from some plan-ahead bulk purchasing. Besides baby supplies, items that will come in handy include paper goods, batteries, film, garbage bags, cleaning products and toilet paper.

Save Sale Finds. During the nine months of waiting, shop the sale racks for baby clothes, bibs, socks and other wearable items that the child will need during the first two years. Think ahead to what size the baby may be during what season. Store all your purchases in a sturdy, under-the-bed storage bin. You can present the entire container to the new mom at her baby shower, or you can use it as a stash of gift items for future holidays and birthdays.

Visit Church Together. New mothers are scared about delivery, whether it's their first or third baby. If you live close by, go to church with them. Let them feel your spiritual love for them. Tell them you are sending up special petitions for the baby. Light a candle with them if the church has them. Help them to feel God's protection. Purchase a cross or other things from the church gift shop with the parents to be for the nursery.

Tour the Hospital. Mom and dad may have a chance to tour the hospital or birthing center as part of their prenatal care classes. Most likely, you will not. Before the blessed day arrives, familiarize yourself with the place where the baby will be born. Write down the address and phone number and keep it in a few places. Know the driving route(s) you will take and where parking is available (as well as how much it costs). If possible, tour the maternity ward, or at least know what wing or floor of the hospital it's stationed. Take note of visiting hours, what's available in the hospital gift shop, and food options for you and/or the new parents. Find out if flowers, gift food baskets, etc. are allowed by the facility and where they should be shipped. Offer to share what you've discovered with family members and friends who are likely to visit the new family in the hospital. Amidst the excitement and stress of getting the call "the baby is coming!" you will appreciate the comfort of having all this information.

❧ Chapter 4 ❦

Mommy Needs Some TLC Too

*J*t's not unusual for the mother-to-be to feel like nothing but a walking tummy at times during her pregnancy. The more she begins to show, the more the focus switches from her as a person to the soon-to-be-born child. You may remember how it felt—strangers wanting to touch your belly and everyone asking if it's a boy or a girl. There may even be a betting pool for the due date! While all this is part of the experience of being pregnant, it can be difficult for some mothers. Without the baby even being born, the spotlight on her individuality is being dimmed. She knows that pretty soon she will be forever known as "Mommy." If she has been a working woman, she may feel this loss of self more acutely.

As her mother or mother-in-law, you can give her the gift of celebrating herself. Spend a little time focusing just on her. What is important is that you are sending the message that she matters to you too, not just the baby. It says something of your commitment to her new role as a parent. Enable her to continue her journey as a woman discovering what life has to offer. Look to provide moments and experiences that offer her a pause from the pregnancy. Strengthening her as an individual has the end result of strengthening her as a mother.

Be a Listening Ear. As the time gets closer, spend more time talking with and listening to the new mom to see what she needs or hopes for in her world. She may have a lot of fears or worries that she needs to share or frustrations that need venting. You can provide the wisdom of your experience and the comfort of companionship as you dialogue.

Pamper Her. There are almost a million ways you can pamper someone; there are ideas that fit everyone's budget. The key ingredients in offering a relaxing and recharging experience are 1) providing the space and time for the new mom to focus on just herself as a person, 2) making sure the activity is something she derives pleasure from, and 3) including a bit of indulgence that makes the experience special and different from the everyday. A spa day complete with a pregnancy massage would be the ultimate, but you do not have to act on that grand a scale. You could treat your daughter or daughter-in-law to a pedicure and stop for a sweet indulgence afterwards. You could send her a "thinking of you" card with a gift certificate to her favorite book store. Or you could simply gift her with a bottle of heavenly scented bubble bath and watch her other children while she soaks in her own bathtub.

Shopping Buddies. Take her out for an afternoon of shopping for clothes that are not pregnancy related. Maternity wear starts to wear on a woman mentally after a while, no matter how fashionable they try to make it. See if she would like a special outfit for coming home from the hospital. Another option is to shop for a few outfits perfect for that "transition time" after the baby is born, when her body isn't ready for her regular wardrobe yet. And should you have a mother who can't stand the idea of shopping for clothes while she is pregnant, consider searching for shoes, accessories, and everyday jewelry together.

Help Her Reclaim Her Figure. Rather than listening to her cry about her weight or how her body looks after baby, help her focus in a positive direction. If the mother wishes, support her in checking out health clubs and exercise programs that she can participate in after the baby is born. Many gyms have nurseries and some offer introductory specials. Discover if there are local mother and baby exercise programs that will let her work out and bond with baby at the same time. In a pinch, an exercise video or an issue of a women's fitness magazine may offer inspiration. (These are available in book stores, libraries and video rental stores.)

Encourage the Family. It may be the case that you are the central point of contact for members of your family to catch up on news of each other.

Encourage siblings and other relatives to relate to the mom-to-be as an individual and call or email for reasons other than to find out "how's the pregnancy going?"

Girls' Day Out. At the end of nine months life changes greatly, and the new mom often has to put relationship-enhancing activities with her friends, co-workers, and/or sisters on hold for a while. Make it possible for her to schedule a girls' day (or night) out so she enjoy those things she won't be able to do as frequently after baby comes. You could organize the outing yourself and make it a day of bonding for all the women in your family, or you could offer to baby-sit her other children so the new mom can have some alone time with her girlfriends. We suggest picking activities that are not baby themed, such as a matinee movie, a paint-your-own pottery session, lunch at that new restaurant, etc.

Foster Her Hobbies. This is essential to her mental well-being, as her hobbies are her passions, and perhaps the last things she wants to give up. You can show your support of her taking this time for herself in little ways. A gift card to her favorite hobby supply store is a wonderful surprise by mail. You could make a gift of a magazine subscription that showcases her favorite interest. Consider joining your daughter or daughter-in-law in her hobbies. It can become a wonderful bonding between the two of you before baby comes.

Just Because Flowers. Send her a fresh smelling bouquet or drop off a flowering plant to brighten her day. Consider delivering her flowers in a keepsake container so she can always remember that you thought of her as a special person in her own right.

Feet Up Day. Give her permission to do nothing for a day. This is an especially nice thing to do when the aches and pains of pregnancy get a body down. Cozy up on the couch together and enjoy a marathon of her favorite DVD movies or TV shows. Treat yourselves to a cooling foot lotion and comfy new slippers. Snack on your favorite foods. You both will be busy when baby comes so enjoy a lazy day together now!

Get a Makeover. Set an appointment at your local department store for a beauty consultation. Share the experience of experimenting with new, exciting colors of eye shadow, lipstick and nail polish. Time this for when the cosmetic counter is offering a bonus offer of a "free gift with purchase" for added value and fun. If makeup is not your thing, or if you want to take this idea further, consider a hair makeover that includes coloring and/or a new hairstyle.

Soothing Sounds. Music can be soothing, energizing, uplifting, and empowering—and definitely personal. Celebrate her uniqueness by gifting her with a CD from her favorite artist or a DVD of their recent concert performance. Don't know what she is currently listening to? A gift certificate to her favorite music shop or online music store offers her the freedom to explore. Don't feel that the only way to gift her with music is to buy it. You could offer to drive her to the local library where she can check out anything that interests her for free.

Tickets to an Event. Scour the newspaper, community bulletin boards or local online calendar for art, music and other entertainment events in your area. Pass the information along with a note saying "thinking of what you love to do" or surprise her with tickets. Some of these showings and performances may even be free! Accompany her if she'd like or offer to baby-sit so she can go with her husband or friends.

Words of Encouragement. Life is challenging enough, and sometimes the hormones of pregnancy make it that much harder to bear. Share with her uplifting words and quotes from a favorite motivational speaker. You will find many fine books, audio books, and magazines available at Christian bookstores. Many are well written by Moms and Dad offering support and advice. Explore the internet to see if you can have an inspirational email or newsletter sent directly to her. At the very least, you can send a card or a bookmark with a saying that inspires.

Add Some Humor. In its extremes, motherhood can be a job you love to hate and hate to love.

Show her the humor of her situation by leading her to a book that celebrates the craziness of being a mother and the fact that you've lost your given name. Erma Bombeck is the classic, but many other contemporary authors provide a good chuckle as well.

Journal. Sometimes all a person needs is the space to think. Provide her with a pretty, blank journal where she can record her thoughts on becoming a mother and on other adjustments she is making to her life. Having such a private, personal outlet can do a world of good. Include an especially nice pen and perhaps a bookmark you've made yourself for that extra special touch. You may even want to include some journaling questions to get her started.

Chauffer Service. Just when you thought your days of driving your children around were over! The last two months of pregnancy make driving difficult for some mothers-to-be (and against doctor's order for some moms who have had C-sections). If you live nearby, offer to drive her around for her daily errands and doctor appointments. It is a kindness that can benefit you both as you share time together.

❧ Chapter 5 ❧

When a Child Is Born,
So Is a Grandparent

*B*abies are just good news. It is said that you love your children but you ADORE your grandchildren. You are about to find out that this is very true. A relationship with a grandchild is heart to heart. Life may dull our eyes, but our ability to see with our hearts gets stronger when a child is around. It seems as we grow older that our steps shorten to just the stride of a child by design. The greatest thing we can give to these innocents, that which they need in abundance, is our wisdom and support.

The range of grandparent relationships is now as diverse as the population. There are many new family situations in which to grandparent, such as adopted grandparenting, step-grandparenting, blended family grandparenting, and grandparenting in a divorce situation. Not to be forgotten are those grandparents who are parenting their grandchildren. There are grandparents who live around the corner and grandparents who live miles away. Whatever your situation, you need not feel alone.

There are many resources available that

provide advice, guidance, insight and suggestions on how you can maximize your grandparenting given your family dynamics. Check for town, city and county programs that are available in your area. Investigate what programs are available at local colleges, vocational schools and through your religious community. National organizations that can offer insight include AARP and The Foundation for Grandparenting. And don't underestimate the internet! With just a little digging you can find a number of grandparenting websites, bulletin boards and interest groups. Learn to reach out to find the support and answers you are seeking—or that you can offer to others.

Define your vision of being a grandparent. What do you wish to make of the experience? How do you want to define your role within your grandchild's life? Take a moment to create the richest, most detailed picture that you can envision. Importantly, touch base with the parents and dream together. Talk about your hopes and ideas for grandparenting. Encourage mom and dad to share their thoughts on the grandparent they hope and wish you to be. This is also an opportunity to discuss boundaries. Share what you will and will not do as a grandparent. Listen to where you will and will not be welcomed. The goal is to start an open and ongoing dialogue, and to build a team. Brainstorm together how the grandparenting and parenting relationships can support each other and create the best environment for the well-being of the child.

❧ Chapter 6 ❧

First Visits and Welcoming Gifts

*Y*ou can't believe the day has finally arrived! You're off to the hospital for a visit or you're meeting the new family at home for the first time. In the rush of emotions and excitement, it can be easy to overlook details that will get your grandparenting adventure off to a good start.

Less Is More. Remember to keep the very first visit short! Unless you have planned things differently with the parents or you are invited to stay longer, try to make the first visit no more than two hours. The new mom is going to be exhausted from delivery and the baby's round-the-clock feeding schedule. Today's maternity wards are hardly the place for relaxing recuperation. Hospital stays are a few days at best—certainly not long enough for a mother to get back on her feet and be the gracious hostess. It's better to come back for a few hours each day of her stay (with her permission) than to visit once for an extended amount of time. This gives you more chances to cuddle the baby!

Shower Her with Flowers. Yes, it may be traditional to send or bring flowers, but it is still a wonderful way to show your affection. Nothing makes a hospital room or home brighter, and studies show that fresh flowers can elevate and enhance a person's mood. The possibilities are endless with today's floral industry, but remember, it is not how much you spend that will matter to the parents but that you remembered at all. Do what you can comfortably afford. If you are delivering the flowers yourself, feel free to create your own arrangement. Placing a potted plant in a child's beach pail decorated with a bow makes a quick and unique gift. (See Chapter 23 for more ideas for creative flower arrangements.)

A Taste of Home. Hospital food does not have the reputation of being the most delicious food on the planet. If you want to be especially kind to the new mom and dad, you may wish to bring some cookies or other favorite goodies for them to munch on during their hospital stay. (Be sure to check if the hospital allows food to be brought in or if mom has "doctor's orders" to follow.) If homemade is not for you, take advantage of supermarket bakeries, sandwich shops, coffee places and restaurants. Another idea is to offer to bring in take-out. Call before you visit to ask if there is anything specifically they'd like you to bring, such as a cup of latte or a made-to-order deli sandwich. Such a simple gesture will mean a lot.

Memento Gifts. You may wish to bring a special gift for the baby to commemorate the birth. This is different than a shower gift, which is generally clothing or equipment geared to make caring for a baby easier. This is a keepsake that is meant to stay with the child—something that gets photographed for the baby album and is cherished for years to come. An item personalized with the baby's name or initials will be sure to bring a tear (most engraving stores can produce such gifts in an hour or two). This is the fun part of grandparenting. Possibilities for memento gifts include:

- a monogrammed blanket with baby's name and birth date.
- a porcelain or collector doll.
- a ceramic bank.
- a musical stuffed toy.
- an engraved piece of jewelry or watch.
- a music box.
- a snow globe.
- a miniature china tea set.
- a commemorative stamp set.
- a collector coin set.
- a porcelain figurine.
- an engraved frame for the first hospital photo.
- a religious article.
- a treat jar with baby's name on it.

- baby's first big truck or big doll.

- a child's rocking chair.

- a keepsake box with baby's name.

Chaperone the Siblings. If the new baby makes someone a big sister or big brother, offer to take the siblings to the hospital to greet the newest member of the family. This gift takes the pressure off mom and dad, and can be an opportunity for you to ease the transition for your existing grandchildren. With the love that only a grandparent can give, reassure the big brother or sister of their place in the family. Help them to get excited about this new, little creature which they'll see as competition for mom and dad's time. This is a great time for spoiling too, especially if you offer a sleepover at grandma's house—something only big boys and girls can do.

A Church Blessing. If your church or the parents' church offers hospital visits (and the parents are agreeable), arrange with the church office to ask for a minister's blessing over the new parents and the baby.

❧ ❧

A baby is born with a need to be loved—
and never outgrows it.

Frank A. Clark

❧ ❧

❧ Chapter 7 ❧

Baby's Home – Now What?

Coming home with baby is not like it used to be. The health insurance industry does not allow long hospital stays in the majority of cases. Moms are no longer spending four days to a week recovering before coming home and jumping back into their "normal" lives. Today's mothers are not hospital-rested; or as mentally and physically strong as they need to be to adjust to a new family routine revolving around the demands of an infant. In addition, many moms have a finite amount of maternity leave—an added pressure to get everything "up and running" before heading back to work.

The truth is, someone often needs to be there the first few days or weeks of mom's return home with the new grandchild. The faster mom gets on her feet, the better it will be for everyone. The transition can be made easier with a little help from a caring party such as yourself.

Ask the new parents what you can do to help! We cannot stress this enough. You are not expected to have all the ideas or to act as a mind reader. Sit down with your daughter or daughter-in-law and brainstorm ways for how you can offer the most love and support during the immediate days and weeks after baby's arrival. Remember, it is better to fulfill one of the new parent's wishes than to provide "help" they won't perceive as helpful.

Consider the following ideas, which you should tailor to your situation and budget.

Be the Baby Nurse. If the parents allow and you are able, make yourself available to act as the "baby nurse." You can be the extra hand they need to help take care of the baby and/or assist with other children. If you can stay overnight, offer to take a nightshift getting up with the baby. Even if mom is nursing, you can help her get back to bed faster if you burp the baby and rock him back to sleep. In the instance where you cannot be there to assist in person, the possibility remains to pay for someone to come in and help.

Watch Her Moods. It's hard to say which is worse—the hormone swings of pregnancy or the hormone readjustment postpartum! Mom is dealing with chemical changes within her body at the same time she's experiencing sleep deprivation. This is a less than ideal situation. Be as reassuring and patient with her during this time as you can be, and encourage other family members to do so too. Mom may be going through a little bit of the baby blues. Be aware of how she progresses through this. As someone who knows her well, you might be able to spot the signs of a more serious postpartum depression before she will. Six weeks after the birth, if she is still struggling, encourage her to talk honestly with her doctor. Work in tandem with her spouse to be supportive if this is the case.

Make a Grocery Run. Offer to do grocery shopping. Taking such a necessary but mundane chore off mom's hands can free her up to rest, bond with baby, or focus on the needs of her other children. Grab her list, coupons and cash, and make the run alone or with dad. If you can be generous as well and cover the cost, it's sure to be appreciated. Resist the temptation to buy items you think should be on the list unless you are absolutely certain they will be welcomed without issue. (It's probably safe, however, to pick up some extra diapers.) Even if you don't live in the same area, you can help. Through the internet you can find grocery and diaper services that will deliver right to the new parent's home. You can even drop a few coupons for baby necessities in the mail.

Wash Up Time. It sounds simple, but it's a biggie to help empty the dishwasher or wash the things in the sink. With the demands of the baby, somehow the sink mess always manages to pile up. This can send a new mom crying, especially if she has been up all night. In less than five minutes, you can help at least this corner of the house stay under control.

Laundry Day. Another fairly easy way to help is to run a load of laundry. Even if you only do the bath towels or the baby's items, it takes something off the list. Usually a newborn goes through its clothing and bedding quickly because of spitting up and leaky diapers. Mom may find that she cannot wait a week to do the baby's wash. Offer to do it for her and put it all away.

Get Baby Out of Her Hair. Sure baby is the center of her universe, but sometimes that is the problem! Mom needs a little time to see to her own needs. Take the baby for a walk in the stroller so mom can shower quietly, return phone calls or take a power nap. Your cuddling and playing with the grandchild in another room can give the new parents time alone to talk and reconnect.

More Food, Please. At this point, the frozen meals prepared in advance of baby's arrival are being depleted. You may wish to make more and send them over. If you'd rather not do the cooking, you can help them purchase some restaurant meals that can be subdivided and frozen for later use. Where before disposable storage/cooking ware was the better option for cutting down on clean up, now you may wish to eliminate their cost by using your durable casserole dishes.

See the Doctor. The first few visits to the doctor's office can feel like a juggling act with all of baby's gear and the wriggly baby. Provide a helping hand for doctor visits—both mother's and the baby's appointments—by tagging along to help carry, watch over and soothe. If mom has delivered by C-section, you may have to drive everyone as well.

Tiny Bubbles. Offer to bathe and dress your grandchild so mom can concentrate on other chores or other children. Who said volunteering to help couldn't be fun? Smile, coo and giggle with your little water baby.

Get Mom and Baby Out. Some moms feel a little house bound after bringing home an infant since the demands of raising baby go round the clock. To help prevent the feeling of tunnel vision, take mom and baby on a short outing. Go for a drive, spend time in a local park or library, or walk laps around the mall for some exercise. The idea is to break the monotony of feedings and diaper changes.

Keep House. The new parents are probably doing all they can do to make a living, care for baby, love their other children, and keep the clutter down to an acceptable level. You can generously provide your time to tackle the light housekeeping that isn't likely to make it on the "To Do" list anytime soon. Wipe down the fridge shelves. Dust the living areas. Put new sheets on the beds. Anything you can do, without making yourself a martyr, will surely be appreciated. Again, get their okay beforehand.

Shine On the Siblings. If the new baby is not the first born of the family, offer to see to the needs of the other grandchildren. Here's a great opportunity to fuss over the brothers and sisters, and remove them from their parents' hair. Give these children special time and treatment as they may be feeling dislocated by the baby's changes to the family dynamic. Shower them with affection, spoil them with love, and help make this a special time for them as well.

෨ ෯

One generation shall praise Your works to another, and shall declare Your mighty acts.

Psalms 145:4

෨ ෯

❧ Chapter 8 ❧

Adoption – A Child Born of the Heart

Since the adoption process takes some time, you may be more than ready for your grandchild's arrival. Adoptive parents come to the world of parenting differently than most. Their struggle to have a child may have involved years of disappointments and sadness. While the journey of each set of adoptive parents is unique, chances are you have shared that journey in some way. Keep your family's particular situation in mind as you welcome the new addition to the fold.

Visiting your new grandchild for the first time will most likely be done at home and not at a hospital. Our advice again is to not make the visit overly long unless you have discussed otherwise with the new parents. Mom and dad are probably tired just from the sheer excitement of it all, and perhaps a bit bewildered by the sudden change to their home life. Another reason to take care that you are not an intrusion is to allow this new family the chance to come together as mother, father and child. No matter the age of the adopted child, they all have to bond. Be loving, be supportive, and be respectful of the new family's needs during this time.

It could be the case that the parents may feel

anxious about your commitment to their adoptive child, especially if you have other grandchildren born naturally. Will you love them all the same? Make sure the parents understand that all your grandchildren will share your heart no matter how they arrived to the family. Reassure them that your heart can love many different people all at the same time. While it may be obvious to you that you would feel this way, stating your thoughts openly may bring great peace of mind to mom, dad, and perhaps someday to your grandchild.

While many of the ideas in the previous chapters still apply in an adoptive situation, you may want to make a special point of gifting something to the child to begin your relationship. A nice touch would be an engraved item that said, "To our Grandson/Granddaughter, love Grandma & Grandpa." If the child is older than an infant, another idea is to make a "Your Family Loves You" poster with pictures of all the family members and their names so the child can see that she is surrounded by a circle of love.

Another idea to help build a sense of inclusiveness is to host an adoption shower after the family has settled in. Invite church friends and family so that the new child feels the support of the loving Christian community surrounds them.

❧ Section II ❧

Be the Best Grandparent
You Can Be

❧ ❦

He who sows sparingly will also reap sparingly, and he who sows bountifully will also reap bountifully.

2 Corinthians 9:6

❧ ❦

☙ Chapter 9 ☞

Spontaneous Grandparenting

*Y*ou can withhold and wait to be asked or you can lovingly offer. That, in a nutshell, is the concept of spontaneous grandparenting.

Our philosophy of spontaneous grandparenting takes the broadest view of what is best for the family—grandchildren, parents and grandparents. It is a selfless approach to grandparenting that empowers you, the grandparent, to make life better for the succeeding generations. Spontaneous grandparenting is about building relationships on a daily basis through little things, rather than just playing grandma or grandpa on holidays and birthdays. At its heart, spontaneous grandparenting is about love freely given without expectations of measured returns.

Depending on the circumstance of your family, choosing to be spontaneous grandparents may mean taking the high road and casting aside wrongs done to you by previous or current generations. You may have the right to say, "Why should I be the generous one, the giving one, when no one did that for me? Why should I be concerned about their well-being when they don't stop enough to think of mine?" We feel that it does not matter if people helped you or not when you were parenting. We also believe in the common wisdom that two wrongs don't make a right. The right thing to do is to change the flaws in the family to write a better future. Your behavior will impact generations to come!

You certainly can recall how difficult and tiring it was to raise your own children at times, and what a relief it was when a parent, friend or neighbor offered to help you with your brood. As a spontaneous grandparent, look for ways to offer that relief without being begged to do so. By lightening the load, you will benefit both your children and your grandchildren. Overworked, tired and emotionally spent parents do not raise their children as well as happy, secure parents. In addition, such frustrations can stress a marriage. You should care enough about your grandchildren to care about their parents. The harried look on mom's face or dad's strained voice over the phone tells you that help is needed, even if they are too proud to ask.

Being a spontaneous grandparent does not imply being a martyr or failing to stand firm on boundaries that you have clearly communicated. It is not intended to make you do things you do not wish to do. Spontaneous grandparenting doesn't mean becoming "the hired help." It does not mean sacrificing all of your time, money and energy. Spontaneous grandparenting is about finding a balance between the extremes that allows everyone to be comfortable in their relationships.

It is easiest to be a spontaneous grandparent when you offer help that takes advantage of your schedule and your talents. Asking "Would you like me to take the little one to nursery school while you are waiting for the repairman?" can be a big help. Or, saying "Would you like me to take junior with me while I go grocery shopping?" can provide a moment's peace in a busy day.

Even if you live too far away to provide help in person, you can still be a spontaneous grandparent. Offer to listen to your grandchild read a book over the phone so the parents do not have to supervise that homework assignment. Send a small toy through the mail to reward a child for a potty training success. Stretch yourself in thinking up ways to show random acts of kindness and support. What may be no sweat to you might bring great relief to busy mom and dad.

Do your part to back up the parents as you practice the principles of spontaneous grandparenting. When the newest generation sees the prior generations working in harmony, it stands as an example for how to build a loving family. With the behavior you model, you can make a lasting impact and communicate your expectations for your family to grow stronger.

Grandma Rosemary shares her thoughts: "When my adult children say to me, 'How can I thank you Mom for all you are doing?' I always answer, 'You'll do it one day for your grandchildren. That is how you will thank me.' I believe in the concept of every generation paying it forward."

❧ ❧

*Our love must not be a thing of
words and fine talk.
It must be a thing of action and sincerity.*

1 John 3:18

❧ ❧

❧ Chapter 10 ❧

Baby-Sitting – Pro or Con?

*B*aby-sitting is probably the most requested help new parents seek. If you speak to seasoned grandparents you will hear many different views on the subject. Everyone has their own preference. As you consider the grandparent relationship you wish to create, it's important that you think about the pros and cons of the issue. Remember it is your choice to sit or not, but weigh your decision carefully.

Some grandparents feel they have waited a long time for their own kids to grow up and will do anything but baby-sit. After all, this is their golden years, their time alone. You need to realize that this position, while valid, may present a hardship on the parents. All parents, especially those with infants and young children, need a break to focus on their relationship (this is good for many reasons, including creating a loving home environment for your grandchildren to grow up in). Trusted child care is often hard to come by. Teenage sitters can be unreliable and inexperienced; professional sitting services can be costly or over their budget. From your children's point of view, having grandma and grandpa watch over their little ones is the next best thing to being there themselves.

You don't want your decision not to baby-sit to come back and haunt you. Many is the story of grandparents who were too busy when their kids and grandchildren needed them, who later found out that no one was there to help them in their older years. Non-baby-sitting grandparents who find themselves in this situation often feel hurt when they learn that the reason their grown children don't want to be there for them is because they felt unsupported during the early years of raising their own family.

If your fears are of being used, then clearly communicate this (preferably before baby arrives). There are grandparents who have been taken advantage of, and left overworked and greatly unappreciated. This is not the situation you want to be in! If you expect a certain level of respect or payback for your kindness, then communicate that nicely. If you are afraid of being turned into the free nanny and worked like a dog, explain your feelings to the parents. It may be that the new parents aren't thinking about the situation from your perspective or have not yet figured out the best way to make the situation work. Remember, this is all new to them too.

One way to keep things from spiraling out of control is to arrive at a joint bartering agreement. Use the words, "I'm glad to help you, but what would make me feel appreciated for my time is if you (state your request)." By stating your needs this way, you allow the parents to decide if your request is doable or not. We suggest that if you cannot arrive at a deal that works for everyone or resentment is built every time you baby-sit, then back out. The grandchildren do not need to have their parents and grandparents fighting.

Open communication is essential, as what help you choose to exchange may need to be revisited from time to time. Also, do not rule out making baby-sitting a financial exchange. Sometimes it can be the simplest way to keep the arrangement fair to all, especially if your baby-sitting rate is less expensive than that of a professional service (this is the kindness you extend as the grandparent).

Another option can be to contribute to a "baby-sitting fund" so the parents can get out once a month. This idea is an especially nice way for out-of-town grandparents and non-baby-sitting grandparents to show they want to help. Let's face it. New babies chew into the family budget so much that often there are no extra dollars sitting around. Creating a special fund for the parents to dip into when they need a breather will benefit your grandchildren by gifting them with relaxed, connected parents.

Don't make the mistake of thinking that baby-sitting has to be an everyday event to be helpful and appreciated. There are grandparents who choose not to or cannot babysit on any kind of a weekly or monthly basis, but who watch the grandchildren for a week or two once a year so the parents can go on vacation. "Camp Grandma and Grandpa" has the dual benefit of creating a happy memory for the children and giving the parents an opportunity to reconnect intimately with each other.

Think of giving not as a duty but as a privilege.

John D. Rockefeller, Jr.

So let each one give as he purposes in his heart, not grudgingly or of necessity; for God loves a cheerful giver.

2 Corinthians 9:7

❧ Chapter 11 ❦

A Personal Note on Baby-Sitting

*W*e feel the greatest gift grandparents can offer is to baby-sit often. The experience can be very rewarding and it often strengthens the family bonds between all the generations. It provides an opportunity to create the relationship you want during some special one-on-one time with your grandchild.

Grandma Rosemary finds that baby-sitting allows her time alone with her grandchildren. "I see it as a gift to myself and not a hardship. I really believe it is my privilege. With the gift of my baby-sitting comes the understanding that Grandma has her own set of rules, and when the kids are in my care at my house that is what we go by. I do spoil my grandchildren when I have them because I believe that every child needs a place that feels like sanctuary—a place where the rules are bent in their favor. I also use the time when we are snuggled up past bedtime to discuss with them their feelings or dreams."

"I try hard to reinforce what the parents do, and I always follow whatever medical stipulations that apply (there are allergies!). But I also have a big colorful Dinosaur cookie jar in the kitchen filled with bite-sized candy. The kids know that if they clean up their mess at Grandma's before they leave then they can pick any treat they want out of the jar no matter what time of day it is. It certainly makes baby-sitting more pleasurable for me if I don't have the dread of cleaning my house every time they leave!"

Mommy Michelle sees allowing her children to have a separate and special relationship with their grandmother as a long term gift. "Naturally, I love when Grandma Rosemary offers to baby-sit, because I do need the time to work and breathe 'kid-free.' And I am certainly lucky to have a mother who savors the joy in grandparenting! But the trick in keeping the situation working for me, and to not see my mother's way of grandparenting as an intrusion into my life, has been to shift my perspective. I keep focused on the gift I am giving to my children when I turn a blind eye to the special treats and softer set of rules. I am allowing them to develop a loving relationship on their own—the first that doesn't involve me or their father. It is my hope that they will take a lot from their time with Grandma and use it throughout their lives. It helps that I have always viewed all my children's grandparents as 'co-parents,' and that I appreciate what each grandparent can offer, rather than demand my expectations."

❧ Chapter 12 ❧

Parenting Then Versus Now

*I*t is hard for people who were so cool in the 50's & 60's to be told that their ways are "old fashioned." If you think your ideas seem dated to your children you aren't going to believe how old you look to your grandchildren! They may equate your life with *Little House on the Prairie* and ask you if you knew George Washington. It is a strange phenomenon and can be upsetting if you are thin-skinned.

The truth is there are still a lot of old time remedies, child rearing techniques, and traditional values that work. You may be totally right in your opinions, but if it is going to cause family strife or be interpreted as meddling, keep your suggestions to yourself. You will find that it is not worth the trouble and that the payoff is dismal if you insist on pushing your way of raising children.

As for the couple's religious beliefs, here you may also be dismayed. There is a beautiful hymn called "Faith of Our Fathers" which for many summarizes what they feel about faith being passed down from generation to generation. We were raised in a day when traditional family values were exercised and handed down. Sadly, the world has changed. Many Christian ways of love and respect are being ignored. Your adult children may not be practicing their faith. Fear not! Silently pray for them. Parenthood has a way of making people grow up fast and it often brings them full circle back to their family's faith.

The situation isn't really about letting go of your children so they can have their own lives and raise their children as they wish—even though your children may view it as such. It has more to do with you spending a lifetime enduring just about everything and developing wisdom that you want to pass on so they can succeed more easily than you did. It's natural to want to share what you know, what you experienced and what you witnessed. You are still a parent, naturally assuming the role of a personal life coach or mentor because you can't stand to see your children hurt and go through difficulties.

But here's the reality. They won't get it any more than we all did when we first became parents. It's that old adage, "The older I got, the smarter my parents became." In the meantime, don't take it personally.

❧ ❧

By the time a man realizes that maybe his father was right, he usually has a son who thinks he is wrong.

Charles Wadsworth

❧ ❧

☙ Chapter 13 ❧

Grandparenting the Toddler Years

*I*t's just you and the baby. Except the baby doesn't stay in one place anymore, has a knack for mess-making, is unquenchably curious, and is developing a mind of his own. Depending on how long it has been since you've been around a toddler, this is either very exciting or somewhat taxing. Most likely, it's a little bit of both.

These beginning years, however, are when you can establish your grandparenting persona. For example, will you teach baby to call you MeMa or Pop Pop? Will you fill a cookie jar with special treats that your grandchild comes to look for every visit? Besides what you can do for and with your grandchild, the toddler years are when you can sprinkle the magic dust of grandparents as liberally as you like.

Here are some suggestions for making the most of these precious years.

Explore Parenting and Family Magazines. Just because these magazines are written for parents doesn't mean they can't offer lots of information and activities for you. The suggestions and tips for keeping toddlers busy and healthy work equally well for mothers and grandmothers. Parenting magazines are also a quick and inexpensive way to become familiar with the "current wisdom" on child rearing. If you don't want to start a subscription, visit your local library for the latest issues or ask your daughter or daughter-in-law to share her magazines when she's done. Most often, these magazines have websites where you can explore a topic, research past articles and print fun activities for the grandchildren.

Just for You. Have a drawer or box of toddler play toys just for the baby. Dollar stores and garage sales can be a source of inexpensive options. Each time your grandchild comes to visit, you can simply pull the box out of the closet and let him explore. Use this as a trick for keeping your grandchild out of the older siblings' toys as well as your own. A toy or two will also work well as a distraction during diaper changes.

Kitchen Band. Take out plastic containers, wooden spoons, metal colanders, etc., and let your little one bang away. Noisy? Certainly. Requires a bit of picking up after? Yes. Encourages a freedom your grandchild might not be able to enjoy in mom's kitchen? Probably so.

Water Play. If the weather is warm, you can indulge your grandchild with some outdoor water play. Simply place a shallow basin on the ground outside and fill it roughly halfway with water. Then toss in empty plastic food containers, funnels, plastic bottles, etc. (certainly nothing breakable or potentially dangerous). Your toddler will love splashing and pouring water from one container to another. As you would with any water activity, stay nearby and supervise for safety. Do not, under any circumstances, leave the child alone.

Natural Explorers. Outside walks make for great bonding time, and toddlers seem to enjoy the unhurried pace of grandparents who let them explore and linger over little wonders. Give the gift of your time by letting your grandchild set the pace. Point out the sights and smells of the world around. Encourage safe exploration, like picking wild flowers and watching caterpillars crawl. Blow bubbles together to see them drift across the sky. You could be the one to awaken your grandchild to the beauty of the world around her.

Baby in the Mirror. The toddler years are when children develop a sense of personal identity. If you can stand little fingerprints, schedule some play time in front of a mirror. It's so cute and funny to watch the youngest toddlers kiss and talk to that "other baby" they see. Placing baby in front of a mirror is a proven technique for calming a fussy toddler. They are often surprised to see themselves looking all red-faced and teary-eyed.

Talk with the Animals. Children of all ages generally love watching, touching and playing with animals. But what do you do if there are no zoos or petting farms within an easy distance? Visit a pet store instead. There's no admission price and purchases generally are not required (though some of the chew toys might be appealing if baby is teething!). Bigger stores will have fish, mice, birds, reptiles, gerbils, etc., in addition to dogs and cats. Depending on store policy, sometimes you can even pet some of the animals. Just make sure that the child has no pet allergies.

Grandma's Library. A cuddly lap and a storybook with lots of pictures make being read to such a pleasure for toddlers. You can help foster a love of reading and of sharing time together by setting up a low bookshelf with a variety of toddler-friendly books. Consider stocking it with books that highlight the special relationship between grandchildren and grandparents. This way story time contains extra lessons about the love between the generations. You will find many exciting faith-friendly children's books, audio, and toys available online and at Christian book stores. Your church gift shop probably carries a fine line of age appropriate learning devices.

My Special Cup and Plate. Invest in a set of plastic toddler-friendly dishes and cups. It may be the same food mommy serves, but to baby it somehow tastes better. Such a simple thing to have—and something all their own—lets your grandchildren know that they are special in your eyes. Remember, like a lot of things, it's all in the presentation.

Cut and Paste. Save your old magazines and kid-oriented catalogs for an afternoon of making collages together. Help your grandchild cut out pictures of things he likes and paste them onto brightly colored construction paper. Encourage your grandchild to share why he chose these pictures as favorites. For this activity, be sure to use non-toxic glue sticks and child safety scissors that can be used by right-handed and left-handed children. To enhance the learning opportunity, challenge your toddler to find pictures that fit a certain category, such as "Animals" or "Healthy Foods."

Spare Clothing. To make it easy on yourself, have two or three extra outfits for your grandchild at your house. (A small bag of diapers or training pants is a good idea to have on hand too.) You can ask the parents to provide them, or pick up some yourself. This way, food messes and diaper leaks don't become a bigger hassle than they already are. Simply change your grandchild's outfit and put the dirty clothes in a plastic bag for mom or dad to launder at home. Request that the spare outfit be returned to you so you're ready for next time.

꙳ ꙳

The kingdom of heaven is like a mustard
seed, which a man took and sowed in
his field, which indeed is the least of
all the seeds; but when it is grown it is
greater than the herbs and becomes a tree,
so that the birds of the air come
and nest in its branches.

Matthew 13:31

꙳ ꙳

꙳ ꙳

Train up a child in the way
he should go,
And when he is old he
will not depart from it.

Proverbs 22:6

꙳ ꙳

❧ Chapter 14 ❧

Teaching Children to Praise God

*T*he greatest thing a grandparent can bestow on a grandchild is a love for God and an appreciation for all He has bestowed on the family. The best way to do this is to let yourself be a living example of God's love and generosity. Encourage your grandchildren to be a part of the Christian world you belong to. Show them you care for God's people and that you have accepted the responsibility of being the light of the world.

Teach them what to "love one another" means by setting the tone in your own family. Discuss with your grandchildren ways they can practice being loving to each other, their parents and their elders. After suggesting a few ideas yourself, such as helping a sibling clean his room (good for younger children) or taking a chore off a parent's list without being told to do so (good for teenagers), encourage them to come up with ideas they can put into action on a weekly, if not daily, basis.

Once the Golden Rule has been established in the family, go out into the community to help those who need aid. Bring to life Jesus' teachings when he instructed "inasmuch as you did it to one of the least of these my brethren, you did it to Me" (Matthew 25:40). As you work as a charitable force within your church and within your neighborhood, have your grandchildren accompany you and help out. Introduce them to your Christian community and all the groups they serve. Let them get involved with you. This may give them a greater appreciation for the blessings in their lives and a way to see more clearly what they should be thankful for to the Lord. Giving of themselves to the community may also help grow their respect for themselves as they see that they can be Jesus to others and make a difference. Your grandchildren will also benefit by seeing you in a different light, outside the role of grandparent, and see another aspect of your life to model themselves after.

Have the children sit down with you and ask for their suggestions for doing God's work. Making them part of the equation will excite them and you may be surprised by their ideas. At the very least, it will teach them to be insightful. It will teach them to look at their world and surroundings differently. Here are some suggestions if you wish to go about doing God's work as a family:

- ❧ Help a Veteran and/or his family.

- ❧ Deliver store bought groceries to a local food pantry.

- ❧ Take children's clothing to a crisis nursery group in town.

- ❧ Bring your used magazines to the hospital's sitting room.

- Donate books to a nursing home.

- Take unopened toiletries to a shelter.

- Do a walk-a-thon for a legitimate national charity.

- Collect spare change to donate to any charity the family is close to.

- Buy new or donate your old books and puzzles to a local, struggling day care.

- Do gardening and yard work for a single mother, widow, or ill neighbor.

- Collect old blankets and towels to bring to the local animal shelter.

Wisdom comes from a long traveled life. It comes from surviving the ups and downs. It comes from knowing your strengths and weaknesses. It comes from understanding your place in the world. It comes from understanding God and all His glory. Share your wisdom with your grandchildren. Tell them of your darkest moments when only God was there to guide you. Explain to them how to look within to survive and how to look above for His aid.

Teach them to pray and be in conversation with the Lord. Have them pray with you for their parents and their schools. Ask them to add petitions for the welfare of others. And pray that your time together will be pleasing to Him. Plant a mustard seed in their youthful hearts and watch your family grow.

❧ Chapter 15 ❧

Grandparenting the Middle Years

*T*his can really be the best of all the times! Potty training and the terrible two tantrums are over. Your little one is much more independent with a growing personality. The ways of interacting are endless and filled with lots of fun. The grandparenting seeds you sowed early on are now starting to show in the relationship between the child and you. They now get excited when you come to visit!

Here are some suggestions for enhancing that relationship during your grandchildren's middle years.

Your Place, Not Mine. Generally speaking, babysitting becomes much easier since your grandchild is capable of helping himself more and is able to follow directions. Now, you may wish to sit more often at the child's home because it is more comfortable for everyone. That's where junior's toys and favorite movies are, as well as all his clothing and comfy bed. As an added bonus, your home stays clean and undisturbed.

Grandma Calling. Even if your grandchildren are as young as three years old, get into the habit of calling and talking to them on the phone. Ask them about their day and tell them that you love them. This plants seeds for the future. If your grandchildren are not used to talking to you on the phone for five minutes weekly, they won't magically begin to do so as teenagers and you will miss hearing about all the accomplishments and joys of their lives then.

Share School Lunch. Many schools allow children to have a grandparent stop in and join them in the cafeteria for lunch. You will most likely find yourself being shown off to a lot of friends! You may also be able to make this an opportunity for a little spoiling by bringing along a favorite treat or providing a few coins to buy chocolate milk. Be sure to ask the parents for permission first before visiting and spoiling in this fashion. If you live out of town, ask the parents if you can supply money for extra hot lunches.

Sponsor or Support Extracurricular Activities. Most parents are super busy, and many are pulled in multiple directions by their multiple children. If you are so inclined, be helpful by taking an active part in your grandchildren's extracurricular activities. You could help a grandson complete a scouting badge or participate at his meetings. You could make paying for dancing lessons a birthday gift or holiday present. If your grandchildren are not involved in organized extracurricular activities, you could teach them a skill or hobby you enjoy instead.

School Spirit. If you have some extra time on your hands, you may wish to join the PTA at your grandchildren's school. Undoubtedly, you probably have a lot to offer having been down that road before. Not only will you make the environment where your grandchildren spend their day better, but you'll be serving the community as well. Your grandchild will love showing you off to all his friends at the next fundraising gala! Helping on a school level will make you part of their life, not just a spectator.

Old Fashioned Game Time. Show your grandchildren how people entertained themselves before video games. You can bring a deck of cards over to play War with them on the front steps. Teach them how to play a wide range of games, such as classic board games, traditional card games, chess, marbles, jump rope and more.

Cookie Baker, Cookie Decorator. Grandmothers and cookies go together like, well, cookies and milk. There are lots of ways to enjoy this traditional activity without you having to become a professional baker. The refrigerated section of the grocery store offers a wide variety of ready-to-bake cookie products. With the help of your grandchildren, add a special ingredient that makes it "your secret recipe," such as mixing in flavored chocolate chips or colorful sprinkles. If you'd rather not turn the oven on at all, you can still enjoy creating something together by decorating store-bought rice cereal squares or plain sugar cookies. A tub of cake frosting and whatever sprinkles or candies you have on hand can be used to create edible masterpieces.

Go Fly a Kite. Kite flying is a simple pleasure and a wonderful way to enjoy a beautiful day. While it's fairly easy to find directions for making a simple paper bag kite in children's craft books or on the internet, you can also purchase inexpensive kites at dollar stores, mass market retailers or discount toy stores. Be sure each child has their own kite as it can be boring watching a sibling fly one while waiting for a turn. Then, head to the nearest wide open space and watch your grandchildren's spirits soar.

Movie Day. This can be tough if your grandchildren are different ages, but sometimes a movie is playing in theaters that's appropriate and appealing to kids of all ages. Treat your grandchildren to a matinee showing, when ticket prices are reduced. If you are afraid of going broke at the concession stand, look for clever ways to split portions. (Considering the size of some movie theater candy boxes and popcorn buckets, this idea is good for waistlines as well as wallets.) Give each child a paper lunch sack that you have cut down to a shorter size and fill it with popcorn from a family size bucket so everyone has some to munch on during the movie. Bring in bathroom-size paper cups and split up a box or two of movie candy. And don't forget to sneak in an old stand-by! Lollipops fit easily in purses or jacket pockets and keep little mouths from talking.

Branch Into the Community. An inexpensive, fun activity can be as close as the nearest parking lot, community park or school yard on the weekends. For example, there are many clubs that meet to race model cars, airplanes, etc., in these locations. Your young grandchild might enjoy watching them, and of course you can always pack a picnic lunch to enhance the experience. Most schools host sport playoffs, art shows and craft fairs a few times a year. Farmers markets or flea markets may be a regular event at a nearby park. Always check the local calendar of events in your newspaper to see what will be going on for the month. You would be surprised! You may spark an interest or feed a passion by exposing your grandchild to any of these activities.

Introduce the Arts. Enriching your grandchildren's lives with the arts need not drain you financially. If you can afford a big city trip or big ticket event, by all means do so. It's an experience neither of you will forget. If the travel and expense of that is too much, look to nearby colleges or high schools. Every year students at these institutions put on amazing plays and concerts that are exciting and fun. You'll be appreciated for supporting the arts at these schools, and you'll also be introducing your grandchildren to their immediate future by showing them what the "big kids" do. The same can be done with high school or college sporting events.

Home Schooling. Any teacher will tell you that students do better and achieve more when their parents are actively involved in their learning. Not every parent, however, can play skill-building games nightly or turn the weekend into an educational field trip. You could use some of the time you spend with your school-aged grandchildren to support their studies and improve their abilities. Have a jar of pennies, nickels, dimes and quarters and go over sorting and counting with them. Play Bingo. Watch a science or nature show together and discuss it afterwards. Do a simple science experiment with them or point out how fractions are used when following a recipe. Even helping with a single workbook page can make your grandchild a better student and show them that you value education.

Shine Your Spotlight. No matter how much attention you shower on your grandchildren, each one needs their special time alone with you. No one believes in us the way our grandparents do! If it's okay with the parents, plan for a one-on-one day with each of your grandchildren in turn. Create a special, age-appropriate day (or weekend) where you focus solely on their likes, needs and talents. Make your granddaughter the belle of the ball or your grandson a king for a day. We're not saying you should let the child dictate, but with a few simple activities and your undivided attention, you can make them feel very, very special. The idea is to make each of them feel like they are "grandma's favorite."

Share Your Passion. If you belong to a choir or church group, let your grandchildren attend a practice or a meeting with you if they are old enough. Seeing you devote extra time to church sends a message. Also, if your parish is sponsoring a special activity for children, ask the parents if you can bring the children. Sometimes it is fun for them to attend a new function or different church and meet new people.

Daydream Together. Sometimes the biggest gift a grandparent can give is a sympathetic listening ear. Find a quiet place, sit back with your grandchild and watch the clouds together. Ask her what shapes or pictures she sees in the clouds and invite her to tell you a story. Share with her the thoughts and dreams you had when you were little watching clouds. Use this time to get an insight into her personality, what she's feeling and what she may be worrying about. It will help you fine tune the love and support you naturally want to give. And should you discover something that the parents need to be aware of—such as a burning passion for horseback riding or a troubling problem with a school bully—be sure to tell them about it. They may not be aware.

❧ Chapter 16 ❦

Creating Traditions

𝒯raditions strengthen the ties between the generations. They are one of the most important gifts to give your grandchildren. Why? Because we live in a global world where few people stay in the same town in which they were born. Families are smaller and divorce is more prevalent. Amidst this mobile and changing landscape, it's challenging to create strong family ties and yet children crave this sort of rootedness.

Undoubtedly, you have a few family traditions that you are looking forward to passing down. If not, many of the fun ideas in this book can be turned into traditions to share with your grandchildren. A tradition begins when a loving activity is repeated time after time to the point that it begins to take on a meaning of its own. It need not be an expensive affair or something done only once a year—though there is a place for those kinds of traditions in our lives (think of Thanksgiving, for example). Sometimes it's the simple pleasures, such as your habit of bringing chocolate donuts every visit, that become the dearest memories to your grandchildren.

In today's world, you might feel that you have to abandon some wonderful old family traditions because time, distance, or both are working against them. This is understandable and prudent. Rather than give them up entirely, challenge yourself to reinvent these traditions to better fit your needs or substitute them with a contemporary activity. The important element to keep alive is not the thing that you do, but what the tradition is centered around or commemorates. For example, if the extended family can't get together on the Fourth of July anymore because of distance or other commitments, perhaps you can have an end of summer gathering instead. The intent to pull the family together, catch up, and celebrate summer is still preserved.

Grandma Rosemary shares: "My mother found that it was impossible to see her three daughters and their families all on Christmas Day. Each year she rotated who she would see and it pained her because we were not all together. So we created a new tradition. The first Sunday before Christmas we all went to her house with our families, exchanged our gifts and shared a meal. Essentially, what we did was move Christmas to another day so Mom could still have us all together for once. And on the actual day of December 25th, we all stayed at our homes with our babies. Mom either stayed with one of us for that weekend or went to visit her brother. This new tradition remained all her life and was a wonderful memory that her grandchildren still talk about."

❧ Chapter 17 ❧

Storytelling

Storytelling is the sister to tradition in creating a tight family. Storytelling is a timeless art that humans have used since language was invented to gather members together, impart important values and morals, teach essential skills for living and foster a sense of unity. It has always been the oldest, most wizened members of the group that carried and shared the stories so they would be passed down.

In the same sense, as a grandparent, you can be a keeper of family stories and the one to make them come alive for the newest generation. Don't think your grandchildren are not interested in learning about what you did "ages ago" or events that passed in the family before they were born. Children, because they are focused primarily on themselves, are often fascinated to learn that other members of the family experienced some of the same things they are going through. Share how you played with your friends when you were their age or share something that made their parents laugh when they were little.

You hold the key to the richness of your family tree. Tell your grandchildren about the "olden days of the 50's or 60's" as well as about their great grandparents, great aunts and great uncles. These people need not be just names recorded in a genealogy book. With your stories about their experiences and life lessons, past generations can become real in the eyes of your grandchildren.

Don't assume that the family knows what you know or that what you know isn't important. It has been proven that family history is often lost within three generations if it is not shared and recorded. Each person's life, including yours, can become a book for future family members to read. You can become the biographer of your family, the minstrel who tells the stories. It's important to do this so that there are no more nameless faces in your family photographs. Wouldn't you want to be remembered, with all that was significant about you, long after you are gone?

Knowing who you are is good for one generation only.

Flannery O'Connor

Certainly don't forget to share your spiritual life story with your family. Tell them about the trying times that God got you through. Tell them about the abundance He has blessed you with. Share your revelations. Teach them about the God who has walked with you every day. Doing this may show your grandchildren how to look within and all around them to witness God's unending love.

❧ Chapter 18 ❧

The Teen Years, aka
What Happened to Baby?

*Y*our sweet little girl or your bright little boy has now grown into an adolescent. These transitional years, when your grandchildren begin to figure out who they are and what path they want for themselves, are still as awkward, emotional and challenging as you remember. Thankfully, teenagers still have a need for grandparents in their lives. You may just have to work a little harder or be a little more creative to find your place in their space.

You may discover that your grandchildren aren't around as much as they used to be, especially if they have a close circle of friends and access to transportation. Those times they are home, you may find them sleeping anytime they're not on the phone or computer! By the time they enter junior high and high school, many teens have social calendars full of parties, sporting events, study dates, team practices, exams, and more. You may find yourself aligned with their parents, who might also be complaining that their teens are too busy or simply uninterested in participating in family activities.

It can be a little disconcerting, and even a bit sad, to deal with the distance your teenage grandchildren seem to be putting between themselves and the family. This is what must be, however, in order for your grandchildren to prepare for the exit from their parents' home that will soon follow. Teenagers seem to need to walk to the beat of the distant drummer they hear. Adolescence is the time your grandchildren will try out all their ideas and teenage costumes (both physically and mentally). And it is better that they do so now, while they are still within the safety net of their family. This experimentation, this development does not mean your teenage grandchildren love you less, even if they don't say the words as freely or as frequently as before.

Phone contact becomes more important now that you are grandparenting teens. This can be an easy transition if you have established a habit of touching base by phone (See Chapter 15 – Grandparenting the Middle Years.) Your teens may really like connecting with you this way since they get to interact with you and still have plenty of time available for school and their friends.

You will find that your grandchildren have plenty to talk to you about as long as you do not pass judgment or lecture them. To guard against this natural tendency (because experience has taught you the error of their ways) be sure you are listening more than you are talking. When you don't agree with something, just add the phrase "well, be careful" said with love rather than cloaked disapproval. Your teens will get it. Your words and tone will tell them you don't agree, but also that you aren't going to hassle them. If what they are sharing really is something grave or dangerous, speak to their parents on a separate phone call. (Asking to speak to their parents immediately after they have shared something they consider intimate will only make them wary and suspicious in the future.) If you maintain a great phone relationship with them during adolescence, it will carry over into college and their young adult years.

Why should you want to hear about the car they are saving for or the prom dress they hope to wear? You want your grandchildren to always be comfortable reaching out to you, no matter what their age. It is important that your teenage grandchildren know that you are only a phone call away should they ever need you. With all the problems facing teens in the world today, it is vital that they have someone they can talk with those times they can't open up to mom or dad.

The phone isn't the only way you can connect with your teen. Plan on attending some of those activities which are keeping them busy. During the teen years, activities almost always translate to a game, recital, school dance, show or award ceremony at some point. Bring your camera and your biggest smile as you applaud their efforts. Don't be afraid to ask your grandchildren directly if you can join them at one of their events. They may have simply failed to invite you because it never dawned on them that you would like to be a part of their busy lives.

If your teenage grandchildren can drive, invite them to visit you on their own now if you live close by and their parents approve. Your teen may discover that mom and dad are more willing to let him drive to see his grandmother than to see some of his friends!

When your grandchildren do come to visit, you can still spoil them even though they may be too old for cheek pinching and cookie jar treats. Take them out alone for dinner or cook them one of their favorite meals. You can also help them financially by paying them do some chores that might be too difficult or tiring for you, such as weeding and mulching or washing the car.

Another gift you can give is the insight to help your teenage grandchildren understand their parents. Teenagers naturally have a lot to say about what their parents do "to them" and what they allow. Never say anything negative about their mom and dad. When your grandchild has a complaint (valid or not), help him to see through it while still being respectful of the parent. Should the situation warrant, you might wish to mediate by talking privately to the parents—either with or without your grandchild knowing.

The teen years are when you can transition into being a mentor and trusted, loving confidant. If you do nothing else but listen, you will be doing a lot. The biggest complaint among teens is that no one really listens to them. As you listen, you can gently guide with only the love a grandparent has. Help them to see that there is life beyond the teen years and encourage them to dream about the big picture for their lives.

Even a child is known by his deeds,
whether what he does is pure and right.

Proverbs 20:12

❧ Chapter 19 ❧

All Grown Up and Leaving Home

*W*hen you first met your grandchild, visions of them as an adult were far, far away. And then you blinked your eyes! Now the time has come for this young person to travel his or her own road.

This is usually a period of adjustment for all. You see your grandchildren happy just as their parents (your own children) become sad. Everyone's role is changing and nothing seems the same. Whereas before the parents and older generations set the program, now more and more is being determined by the youngest generation's schedule. Traditions become modified or abandoned sometimes. The parents may not show up at your home on holidays anymore so that they can rush off to visit their children at college or their new apartment or home. It is also a time when in-laws enter the picture as your grandchildren marry and have babies of their own.

The transition can be difficult when you've been accustomed to being so involved with your children and grandchildren. Yes, it's great to not have the house get messy anymore. Yes, your bowling score may improve now that you can get to the lanes more often, and most of your needlework finally will be completed, but it is hard to ward off the devil of nostalgia. It will rear its head at the most inopportune times, while you are sitting in the park, or shopping in the mall, or driving by the school playground. Watching scenes that used to be the mainstay of your life can bring a tear to your eye. How do you replace that kind of love? The truth is you don't; and it is upon this realization that you know you have succeeded. Uncaring, detached people don't ever feel this.

It is a time for you to redefine your life again knowing that the future will bring new joys and adventures. You may begin the transition from grandparenting to great-grandparenting before you know it! (Don't worry, a lot of ideas from this book still hold true.) Destiny has more to unfold and you will arrive with greater wisdom than ever before. A lifetime worth of memories with your grandchildren have made it all worthwhile.

છે જી

Creative thinking may mean simply the realization that there's no particular virtue in doing things the way they have always been done.

Rudolf Flesch

છે જી

❧ Chapter 20 ❧

Where Did Everyone Go?

*W*ith the evolution of your grandchildren into adults, you may feel at times like a lonely grandparent. The love is there, but the grandchildren and extended family, being propelled into new directions, may not express it as frequently or make time to act upon it. If you feel that you've been put on the back burner because they are so busy, then this is something you should convey to your family in the nicest of terms.

For some grandparents, this situation is a welcomed relief; for others, not so much. Talk with enough grandparents and you will hear over and over how many don't want to go back home to visit because the grandchildren spend only ten minutes with them and the parents are too busy running after the kids. Many people feel it is not worth the expense of driving or flying home if they are not going to see much of their family. The situation leaves them feeling unwanted and facing some tough emotions.

Be proactive to save yourself from feeling this way. Remember that you are still their family and it is all right to state your needs. Gracefully say, "I'd like to come and visit if you have some quality time for me. If not now, when is a good time?" Good relationships are built on honesty.

Focus on what you would like to achieve with the visit. What matters to you most? Is it visiting with each of your grandchildren separately or do you prefer to have a big extended family gathering that everyone agrees to attend? Communicate your wishes and preferences with love and even a bit of humor. Be open to compromise and work toward a solution that will make your time together memorable. By behaving in this fashion, you will teach the entire family that change can be a positive experience for everyone.

❧ ❦

Too many people miss the silver lining because they are expecting gold.

Maurice Setter

❧ ❦

❧ Chapter 21 ❧

The Gift of Good-Bye

*I*t would be a disservice to fail to address a situation that exists for a lot of grandparents. For a whole host of reasons, the family is at odds. You, and your ideas about grandparenting, may not be welcomed at all.

Maybe you had dreams of being an involved, hands-on grandparent and you were told otherwise by your children. You may be separated from your adult child or you do not get along with their spouse. Or together they may not get along with you and you are not really sure why. This can be very hurtful and undoubtedly you have spent nights crying about it. It's another reminder that life is not always fair.

If the parents knew how much they were denying their children, whom they say they love, they would not be keeping you from your grandchildren. But, right or wrong, that may not be their mindset. You can try writing a loving letter but it may be rebuffed. Sadly, there may be nothing you can do about it. The more you try and force the situation, the worse it will probably get. You may have to let it be, kiss it up to God, and hope the situation improves in the future.

You are not alone if you have grandchildren you are barred from seeing. It is only right to mourn the ones you are kept from, but it would be a disservice to the grandchildren you do see if you let these feelings effect your relationship with them. They should be loved and praised for being by your side and should not have to see you cry for those who are not there. Be happy for what you have and do not grieve about what is missing. You will be a much better grandparent that way.

If you are a good person, you know that in your heart. God sees all. Rest assure that He feels your pain. You know what you could have done and the difference you could have made in everyone's lives. Know it is your adult children's loss and constantly remind yourself of that.

Should you find yourself in this situation with your only grandchild, you may want to fill the void by volunteering at a crisis nursery in your area or with a service club that caters to the needs of children. Your misfortune may be a calling to help a child that has no one. If you are good at nurturing, your gift can make the difference in another child's life.

Sadly sometimes the best thing you can do is to give your adult son or daughter the gift of good-bye. It hurts, but fighting at every holiday and saying awful things in front of the grandchildren is not right. These are not the memories you want your grandchildren to have.

Many grandparents have seen their adult children return after a time. In the meantime, live your life to its fullest. It might make you feel better if, for each grandchild, you put aside a box to fill over time with the trinkets and little notes you would have gifted. One day, you may have the opportunity to hand it to them should they show up at your door seeking you out or if the family reconciles.

Our all-knowing God sees the desires of your heart. If there is a way to unite your family, He will deliver it. He will bring forth his angels to reach everyone and soften their hearts. His will is always done. He is the God of miracles. Now more than ever, you must have faith and trust in God. The time of discord will feel long but perhaps that is the path God wants everyone to go down.

Say a prayer for the prodigal children and ask God to help you with your broken heart.

❧ ❧

It was right that we should make merry and be glad, for your brother was dead and is alive again, and was lost and is found.

Luke 15:32

❧ ❧

❧ Section III ❧

Ideas for Active Grandparenting

๛ Chapter 22 ๛

Ideas for Hosting a Baby Shower

*A*s the grandmother, you most likely will be involved with the baby shower for your grand-child-to-be. Baby showers are very similar to bridal showers in that they gather a group of people around the person of honor to shower her with gifts and warm wishes.

In today's world, because of distance, work schedules and equality of the sexes, the nature of baby showers has changed. It's perfectly acceptable for the new mom to have more than one shower. She might have one with family and friends, another with her co-workers in her office, and possibly another through the mail involving her out-of-town friends and relatives. Couple showers have also become popular, where the friends of the new mother and new father are invited and both parental roles are celebrated.

Be prepared that as the grandmother you may be invited to more than one baby shower even if you are hosting your own. Don't feel that you are limited to attending one event. Enjoy each shower you are invited to, if it is comfortable for you to attend. Now is a good time to meet the people who are closest to the new mother as they most likely will be a part of the baby's life. (Think ahead to who's going to be at all the birthday parties, play groups and backyard barbecues.)

For the baby shower you are hosting, work with the new mother. Ask her to share her thoughts and feelings concerning the party. Does she want a traditional baby shower set at home or does she want something different? Is her mother or mother-in-law also hosting a shower of which you need to be considerate? You and the new mother may both have lots of ideas for your party. Remember to compromise and keep in mind that it is her shower. It may be best if you agree to a budget and the guest list before you start planning anything else.

Baby showers are usually hosted in the mom's sixth, seventh or eighth month. Any earlier is not appropriate and any later means you run the risk of not having the party if the baby comes early. Generally, baby showers are not a surprise, but planned dates. They are a big help to most couples because it helps them get the things they need for the baby.

Baby Shower Party Possibilities

  Host a small event at your home or favorite café featuring a special luncheon buffet. If hosting the party at home, you can cook all or some of the items yourself or have the event catered.

  Plan a simple party with a beautiful cake and an indulgent tray of cookies. Serve a selection of beverages, such as coffee, tea or punch in elegant glasses.

  Have a casual gathering in the backyard with deli-made trays of sandwiches and sides. Another option is to serve a 3-foot long sub.

  Enjoy a formal tea party with fine china, platters of tea sandwiches, delicate pastries and a variety of flavored teas. Use a large coffee urn to heat and hold hot water.

  For a gathering of close friends and family, invite guests to contribute a dish for a potluck. Consider asking each person to share the recipe for their dish or to bring a recipe the new mother can easily cook while managing her baby.

  Host a "baby shower by mail." You set a date giving the guests at least four weeks to shop or order from the stores at which the new parents have registered (encourage them to create some online baby registries too). Everything should arrive about the same day to the new mom. Take a picture of mom with each gift to send as part of her thank you notes.

❧ Have the shower at a themed restaurant, such as a Japanese teppanyaki house where the food is cooked tableside or a fondue restaurant. Have everyone pay their own way and take a collection in advance to present one big gift from the group. The shower then becomes a fun night out for everyone.

❧ If the shower is for a second or third child, consider a library theme since the parents already have a lot of baby equipment and hand-me-down outfits. Ask the guest to bring a beloved children's book to start a library of favorites for the new baby and perhaps a book on parenting (factual or humorous) for mom or dad to enjoy.

Baby Shower Activities

❧ Include a Baby Wishing Well. This is where a laundry basket or small wagon is set up and, in addition to their regular gift, guests bring an extra "wishing you well" gift such as baby shampoo, baby wipes, booties, bibs, sippy cups, etc. Wishing well gifts are generally small items that don't cost more than a few dollars. Their value adds up, however, and their practicality is greatly appreciated!

☙ Place a child's bank on a table with the sign reading "College Fund" and invite everyone to contribute their loose change. This idea works best in a circle of close family and friends not easily offended.

☙ Create a sign-in book or scrapbook page and ask guests to share a tip for the new mom or a special wish for the new baby along with their signature. You could also create a "my prayer for you" page.

☙ With the mom-to-be, decide upon party games that fit your theme and if you plan on awarding prizes. Some suggestions include word scrambles, guess the flavor of baby food, baby trivia and guess the number of jelly beans in a baby bottle. Lots of wonderful ideas for shower games can be found on the internet and in parenting magazines and books.

☙ Give each guest a decorative index card and ask them to write a note to the new baby offering general advice on "how to live life." Let people be as humorous or inspirational as they like. Afterwards, collect the cards and keep them in a special memory box to share with the child when he's older.

☙ Ask guests to bring an item to include in a time capsule that is filled during the party. You may want to include a list of suggestions with the party invitation. (Some baby and party stores carry time capsules kits in case you do not want to create one yourself.)

❧ Invite guests to decorate white baby onesies with fabric markers, rhinestones, iron-ons and whatever else you want to provide. If you use onesies in different sizes, baby can showcase this wearable art throughout her first year. The same idea can be applied to bibs, burp cloths, hats and socks. (Make sure to use cardboard inside the onesie to prevent bleed-through while decorating.)

❧ Purchase already fired ceramic items from your local craft store that can be decorated with permanent markers. Options include banks, figurines, mugs and plates. Purchase a variety for the party so each guest can choose an item to specially decorate for baby. Make available a range of colored permanent markers, rub-on designs, rhinestones, etc.

❧ Chapter 23 ❧

Ideas for Stocking the Freezer

*W*hen baby first comes home, so much attention and time is consumed by her care that healthy, economical meal planning and preparation can fall by the wayside. One of the greatest gifts you can give is helping with meals and kitchen care so the adults are well fed. Otherwise, the tired parents may resort to breakfast cereal or peanut butter and jelly sandwiches for dinner more times than not!

The numbers of pre-made meals you can supply are endless. The challenge is to look at any cookbook recipe and see how you can modify it for freezer storage and reheating later. The goal is to make it easy for the parents to feed themselves and avoid having a big mess afterwards to clean up. Babies often fuss during the dinner hours, no matter what you do. After a long day, this can bring the new mom to tears and frustrate the new dad.

Bringing over some freezer-friendly meals not only helps the new parents eat but teaches them something as well. They can learn from your example and figure out what meals they would like to cook and store in advance for nights when they are pressed for time or lack energy. They can begin to see that a little bit of smart planning will save them time and money.

Ideas For Cooking, Storing, Transporting, and Reheating

- ❧ Invest in a bunch of plastic food containers for storage and transportation of your meals. You can even save the ones deli meats come in from the grocery store. You will be cooking in bulk and dividing it into meal size portions for later use. (Make sure to check if you can freeze, microwave and/or bake in these containers before doing so.)

- ❧ If cooking from scratch is not your forte, substitute as many precooked, ready-to-use ingredients in your recipes. For example, try frozen meatballs as a base for a meat stew, refrigerated grilled chicken strips in a pasta Alfredo, or ready-to-heat microwavable rice to mix in a casserole.

- ❧ A rotisserie chicken is an economical and quick meal in itself. Many grocery stores prepare them fresh daily. They are also a great starting point for creating other dishes. There are several cookbooks on the market on just this subject.

- ❧ From the cooking pot, place foods in disposable containers made for reheating in the microwave and/or oven. Place the filled containers in your freezer until you have prepared all that you planned. Use a cooler to transport your meals between homes to keep items frozen.

ڸ Be sure to communicate your plans with the new family and make sure they have room in their freezer to store all the foods you bring.

ڸ If you are known for a particular dish and it is a favorite of your child, you might want to prepare it as a treat for them. They are apt to appreciate this special love and attention from you.

Ideas for Easy, Freezer-Friendly Meals

ڸ Purchase pre-made frozen stuffed shells. Portion into containers and cover generously with prepared spaghetti sauce or with canned tomato sauce to which you have added some chopped fresh basil and grated parmesan cheese. Send along a box of frozen garlic toast to complete the meal.

ڸ Prepare four boxes of flavored rice mix according to the package directions. To this, add 2 cups of a favorite canned vegetable and 1 cup diced chicken, cubed ham, or diced cooked sausage. Divide into four casserole sized containers.

ڸ Prepare four boxes of your favorite macaroni and cheese product according to the package directions. Divide this among four casserole sized containers. Turn each container into a different meal by mixing in a variety of ingredients. Suggestions include:

- ❧ One to two cans of shrimp and one can of quartered artichoke hearts packed in water. (Drain all cans before using.)

- ❧ Half pound of cooked ground turkey, chicken or veal. Top with seasoned breadcrumbs and parmesan cheese.

- ❧ Half pound cooked ground beef browned with one tablespoon of chili spice mix (spice can be adjusted more or less to your taste) and ½ cup of chopped onions.

- ❧ Make a vegetable barley soup by combining two cans of chicken and vegetable soup, two cans water, ½ cup canned diced carrots, one small can of sliced mushrooms and 1 cup quick cook barley. (Drain all cans before using.) Cook for 15 minutes or until the barley is tender. Thicken the soup by sprinkling in instant potato flakes if desired.

- ❧ Make a meatloaf mixture by combining two pounds of ground beef with one pound of ground pork or ground veal. Add approximately one cup of Italian seasoned breadcrumbs, ¼ cup of grated parmesan cheese and some water to moisten. Form into small loafs and place into individual disposable tin loaf pans. Cover each tin with foil and bake at 375 degrees until almost done. Drain off some of the fat from each pan. Then pour enough jarred spaghetti sauce to cover each loaf. Bake uncovered for an additional 10-15 minutes. Let the meatloaves cool and recover each with the foil before freezing. Each loaf can be served as a meal or sliced for meatloaf sandwiches.

ॐ Create a simple slow cooker beef stew by combining one large bag of frozen mixed vegetables, two pounds of stew meat cut into bite-sized chunks, one can of cream of mushroom soup and one cup of water or beef broth. Cook on low for three to four hours. Season with salt and pepper to your own taste. Thicken the stew with a sprinkling of instant potato flakes if desired.

ॐ Purchase a package of individually frozen breaded chicken strips or patties. Brown in pan with 2 tablespoons of olive oil. When almost cooked, add ¼ cup bottled lemon juice and ¼ cup jarred capers. Cook until this liquid is reduced by half. For a brighter lemony taste, substitute the bottled lemon juice with one tablespoon of zest and the juice from one fresh lemon mixed with one teaspoon of cornstarch.

➷ Chapter 24 ✄

Ideas for Creative Floral Arrangements

𝓕lowers are a traditional gift when welcoming the news of a new baby. Besides bringing an arrangement to the hospital to congratulate the family, floral arrangements are also appropriate when the mom initially shares that she is pregnant, when decorating the room for the baby shower, and when mom is feeling especially tired during the ninth month. Flowers are even a nice gift for a granddaughter, especially when celebrating religious or school achievements and special birthdays.

You don't need to be a florist to put together a beautiful arrangement. Many grocery stores sell fresh flower bouquets and craft stores offer a wide assortment of vases and decorative containers in addition to silk flowers and plants. With a little creativity, you can create a memorable flower gift that costs far less than buying one from a professional floral service.

Floral Arrangement Ideas

➷ Use a cookie jar as a vase. Tie a bow around it and fill it with fresh flowers.

- Choose a pretty ribbon to tie a small rag doll or stuffed animal to a clear vase filled with fresh flowers.

- Purchase a live green plant and add a few silk flower stems to it.

- Rest a small pink or blue basket filled with silk daisies on top of a tin of cookies.

- Place an ivy wreath (fresh or silk) on top of a wood serving tray and place a pink or blue candle in the center of the wreath. All three items can be enjoyed separately long after the need for the arrangement passes.

- Fill a cut glass champagne bucket with a bottle of sparkling wine or non-alcoholic beverage, two champagne flutes and a sippy cup. (The wine is intended for mom and dad only, of course!)

- Use a child's sand bucket to hold a box of animal crackers, baby sun block, a beach hat and a large silk sunflower or two.

- Place a bouquet of fresh flowers in a china tea pot with a beautiful floral pattern.

- Wrap a baby blanket or bath towel set around a large bouquet of fresh flowers, and tie with a big ribbon. (Wrap the flower stems in a plastic bag to prevent water leakage.)

- Use a keepsake photo memory box to hold a potted orchid. Tuck a disposable camera inside the box too.

- Place an assortment of baby shampoos and lotions inside a baby bath designed to fit in a sink. Decorate with silk ivy branches and scattered pink or blue silk flowers.

- Tie some mylar balloons to a wicker basket holding a live green plant.

- Use a large glass fishbowl vase that has a top piece for a plant. Fill the vase with layers of pink and white or blue and white jelly beans. Then take a small spray of silk flowers and arrange in the planter section.

❧ Chapter 25 ❧

Ideas for Spontaneous Grandparenting

𝒶s mentioned previously, the concept of spontaneous grandparenting requires a special relationship between the generations and works only when the parents give their permission. Since spontaneous grandparenting can be viewed as a form of co-parenting, it is crucial that the parents and the grandparents work as a team and decide together on what help is needed, offered and accepted.

If the parents invite your help, here are suggestions that you may be willing to offer to make spontaneous grandparenting a successful part of your life.

- ❧ While you are doing your grocery shopping, call and ask the parents if they need a few items.

- ❧ Offer to drive your grandchild (one way or round trip) to one of his after school activities, such as scouting or sports practice.

- ❧ When possible, schedule your errands to coincide with your grandchildren's activities so you can easily stop by and view their dance or karate class. This shows your grandchildren how proud you are of them.

- ❧ Meet the kids at the bus stop so that mom can stay out a little longer running her errands.

- ❧ Go with the parents while they are shopping and keep the baby distracted so they can concentrate on their list.

- ❧ Offer to pick up your grandchild from day care, nursery school or grade school. (Be sure your name is included on any security lists these schools may require.)

- ❧ Do a school project with your grandchild to give the parents a break and the student another mentor to learn from.

- ❧ Remove a child-centered errand from the parents' list. For example, take your grandson shopping for new sneakers or your granddaughter to the mall to get new ballet tights.

- ❧ Take the kids to the library and show them how much you enjoy reading. Be endearing and read whatever children's books they bring to you.

- ❧ Every so often, offer to baby-sit so the parents can enjoy a date night. You may wish to bring dinner for the kids also to make it easier for mom and dad to get out of the house.

❧ If you can afford it, check clearance departments at stores and pick up what the kids can use since the parents' budget may be tight. Gifts for no reason are very helpful!

❧ Your grandchildren are certain to have a favorite character or a liking for a certain type of item, such as action figures, costume jewelry or teddy bears. Every so often, gift them something that goes with this passion. It's a great opportunity for fun spoiling and for being sweetly remembered for purchasing something they especially love.

❧ Work on adding to your grandchild's special collection, may it be rocks, trading cards or a children's book series.

❧ Send your grandchildren "Thinking of You" cards addressed to them directly. Kids love receiving their own mail! You may wish to congratulate them on a special achievement such as a good test score or a dental visit with no cavities.

❧ When your grandchildren come to visit, display a few pieces of their artwork in a prominent place in your home so that they can see how much you treasure their talents. Another idea is to keep them in a large binder so you can flip through the pages together.

∾ Get the children up and off the couch! Play simple lawn games with them, such as catch, croquette, horseshoes or badminton.

∾ Create a special treasure box for each grandchild that has their name on it (you could invite them decorate a shoe box). Place inside it a few pieces of candy, some stickers, a few coins and little love notes from you. You'll all look forward to opening it each visit.

∾ Invite your grandchildren to teach you something—from board games to video games. They will enjoy the role reversal and you may learn a fun thing or two.

∾ ∾

Give a little love to a child,
and you get a great deal back.

John Ruskin

∾ ∾

ᔥ Chapter 26 ᔥ

Ideas for Gift Giving

*T*here are many occasions to celebrate with your grandchildren. In addition to all the birthdays and holidays, there will be many achievements and milestones to be commemorated through the years. There are also certain to be times when you'll wish to do something special to reward and encourage positive behaviors. Here are some ideas, big and small, for ensuring your gifts are loved and memorable.

Gifts For Girls or Boys

ᔥ A gift box containing a photo album or scrapbook, an assortment of stickers, a pen and labels, and a disposable camera so that your grandchild can take and keep pictures of the things that are important to them.

ᔥ A saucepan, ladle and packages of higher-end soup mix make a great cooking lesson for a middle school or older child. You may wish to include a beginner's cookbook, or the recipe for a soup or other dish that you are known for making.

ؘ A glass jar you've decorated or a whimsical ceramic cookie jar filled with teething biscuits for a baby or pre-packaged snacks for an older child.

ؘ A big mug filled with individual packets of flavored hot cocoa and mini-marshmallows. Combine this gift with a new scarf and glove set for the perfect winter-time present.

ؘ For a high school or college bound child, a desktop basket filled with a pocket-sized dictionary and thesaurus, a blank journal, and a decorative pen will certainly come in handy. You may even want to include some stamped note cards pre-addressed to you!

ؘ A large, inexpensive plastic bowl filled with packages of microwaveable popcorn. Choose all different flavors, and consider adding shakers of different popcorn seasonings. You can also include a DVD movie or a gift card to a rental store.

ؘ A small picture frame or decorative ornament that can hold a special school picture or sport photo. You can even personalize it using a permanent marker.

ؘ A grooming hygiene kit for traveling and sleepovers with friends that includes a toothbrush and paste, comb and brush, travel-size soaps and lotions, hand sanitizer, etc. For an older child, you could include a small bottle of perfume or cologne.

&ice; A shirt or other article of clothing to which you've sewn on cute buttons, ironed on patches or customized with the child's name.

&ice; A year's subscription to a child or teen magazine to encourage their learning and hobbies.

&ice; An overnight tote bag for going to Grandma's with plenty of space for bringing a favorite toy, stuffed animal or blankie. You could even include a new a pair of pajamas inside.

&ice; Bundle a monogrammed beach cover-up or towel with a pair of flip flops, sunglasses and sunscreen. Everything could be placed in a large beach bag or pail.

&ice; A DVD movie or video game with a matching book and T-shirt.

Especially For Girls

&ice; A jewelry box that contains her first piece of jewelry from you. Through the years, you can add pieces to build her collection. Think affordable jewelry or consider passing on little worn jewelry of your own to make this tradition easy to continue.

- Fill a fancy hat box (easily found in craft stores) with hair bands, barrettes, and bows for a pretty gift that also keeps everything organized.

- A locket engraved with a special message from you (including your name) on the back. You could also include a picture of you and your granddaughter together to go inside.

- A pretty lined basket filled with dance wear or princess clothing. Check clearance bins, dollar stores and thrift stores for inexpensive costume jewelry.

- A jean purse or a plain tote bag filled with fabric markers, puffy paints, and a stencil or two for your granddaughter to use to create a fashion statement. You could even include a plain white T-shirt or two to decorate.

Especially For Boys

- A canvas box that you've personalized with your grandson's name using fabric marker or paint to hold all his miniature cars, trains or action figures. Include a new toy for his growing collection as well.

- A sturdy photo box filled with trading cards. You can add a few packs of cards to the collection every time your grandson has done something well.

- A watch engraved with a special message from you (including your name) on the back.

- A baseball cap or T-shirt featuring their favorite sport team along with tickets to a game. If tickets to a professional event are too costly, consider getting seats to a high school or college game.

- A tackle box filled with all the necessities along with a note promising to take them fishing.

The manner of giving is worth more than the gift.

Pierre Corneille

ప Chapter 27 ప

Ideas for Vacationing
with Grandchildren

$\mathcal{V}$acationing with the grandchildren can be the greatest fun! You can explore a variety of ways to spend time together. You can choose to be a part of an extended family vacation that includes mom, dad and the grandkids, or you can invite your grandchildren to stay with you while their parents get away. No matter how you arrange vacation time with your grandchildren, there are easy ways to make it fun and memorable for all of you.

You can encourage your grandchildren's anticipation by talking about your vacation plans by phone in the weeks or months before the trip. Ask them what they hope to do or see. Besides giving you the opportunity to know more about their personality, it may give you clues about what to plan to make the vacation more fun.

Ideas For Vacationing At Grandma's and Grandpa's Place

ప Take them to see your friends and let them hear all your stories.

- Visit local museums and historical sites of interest.

- Spend a day at a local fair or traveling circus.

- Explore a farmers market and pick up some wonderful foods to cook together.

- Visit a local petting farm or nearby zoo.

- Attend a church event together, such as a potluck dinner or charity bazaar.

- Plan a picnic in the park or backyard, complete with lawn games.

- Take them to a drive-in movie if one is available in your community.

- Enjoy an afternoon bowling and then celebrate at an ice cream parlor afterwards.

- Enjoy the great outdoors together with a nature walk along a nearby trail or a visit to a state park.

- Plan an afternoon of water activities, whether that means running through the sprinkler or spending time at the community pool or beach.

- Make an outing of playing miniature golf, or create a course of your own together in the backyard.

- Have a "make your own pizza" night. Each grandchild can add their favorite toppings to an individually-sized pizza or a section of a communal pizza pie. (Fresh pizza dough and pre-baked pizza shells are both available at grocery stores.)

Ideas for Extended Family Vacations

ళ Take the grandchildren hunting for sea shells while the parents enjoy swimming or lounging in the sun.

ళ Baby-sit young grandchildren in the hotel room at nap time. This gives you time to rest too.

ళ Cook a meal if your guest room has a kitchen or go to the hotel café with the kids so mom and dad can enjoy dining alone.

ళ Help to distract children or play with them during stressful or boring times of the vacation, such as during hotel check-in and out, waiting in line, unpacking and packing, and airport delays.

ళ Escort your grandchildren to the activity center or game room at your resort. Reward good behavior with a few extra coins or tokens.

ళ While the parents shop, take the kids to another area of the store or mall that interests them. Find a discount store for them and hand them a few dollars to spend on anything they want.

- Bring along a tote bag filled with kid-friendly items to help quiet the children. Pack small packages of snacks or sweets, dollar store toys, coloring supplies, a deck of cards and other items that can keep mouths closed and hands busy. Dole these goodies out throughout your trip.

- Stroll the baby while the older kids and adults enjoy the theme park thrill rides.

- Ask everyone to pack jeans and a white shirt, then pose together for family pictures. Have mom or dad get a few of you surrounded by the grandchildren. You can ask another guest or resort employee to take a picture of the whole clan.

❧ Section IV ❦

A Final Thought

❧ Chapter 28 ❧

If Grandmothers Ruled the World

*W*hat kind of world would it be if grand-mothers ruled the world? Could we find a group of people any more caring and insightful? Many people can attribute their own success to the love and guidance of a grandmother. The wisdom of our grandmothers can truly be the air beneath our wings.

Like the old song says, "If I ruled the world, every day would be the first day of spring...." In that vein, wouldn't it be a wonderful world if grandmothers had their say?

If grandmothers ruled the world ...

- ❧ Homemade chicken soup would be on the school lunch menu every day.
- ❧ Everyone would have a warm scarf knitted in their favorite color.
- ❧ There would be 50% more kisses and hugs.
- ❧ Bullies would not exist.
- ❧ We would celebrate our birthdays every month on our special day.

- No child would ever be lost.
- Naps would be required.
- Church would always be full on Sunday.
- Penny candy would no longer be a memory.
- Pets would live forever.
- The choir would never sing off-key.
- Stories would always have a moral.
- There would be no tears.
- You could eat all the ice cream, cookies and cake you wanted, and never gain an ounce.
- It would never take "forever" to finish homework.
- Everyone would have a listening ear to turn to.
- Toys would put themselves away.
- Every bake sale would sell out.
- Small fortunes would be made with lemonade stands.
- You would always receive a timely thank you card.
- Memorizing the 23rd Psalm would be part of every child's education
- You could sleepover at grandma's whenever you wanted.

- You could sneak whole meals into the movie theater.

- Bubble gum would never get stuck in hair.

- Saying "be quiet" or "stop fighting" would work like magic the first time.

- All boo-boos would be healed by kisses.

- People would understand that the greater joy is in giving, not receiving.

- Every story would have a happy ending.

❧ ❧

Let the little children come to Me,
and do not forbid them;
for of such is the kingdom of heaven.

Mathew 19:14

❧ ❧

FROM NOTHINGNESS...BEAUTY

Like a beautiful cathedral
Put where empty space once stood,
Like a warm and hearty campfire
Made from useless sticks of wood...

Like Springtime's budding flowers
Awakening from the cold
To blossom into beauty
With colors green to gold...

Like a skyscraper erected
From tons of stone and steel,
As a testament to Mankind,
Built with strength and zeal...

Like a portrait put to canvas
With a sure and steady hand,
Inspired from within to make
A masterpiece that's grand...

So, too, our lives are fashioned
By the Lord our God above,
Into creatures in His image,
Filled with faith and hope and love.

So we owe it to ourselves and Him
To live as best we can,
To glorify and honor Him
And love our fellow man,
So that when He comes to call us-
Our lives at least complete-
We can look behind without regret,
And ahead to a Heavenly seat.

- Mike Weis

❧ The Authors ❧

Rosemary Weis is a mother of six children and a grandmother many times over. She's pioneered town-wide enrichment programs for elementary and middle school students, has written a children's Christmas tale, and has extensive volunteer experience working with a number of children's charities. She currently resides in the Orlando, Florida area where she's working on several book projects. She also keeps a magnet on her refrigerator that reads "My favorite people call me Grandma."

Michelle Johnston, with her three children, is happily responsible for elevating Rosemary Weis to the title of Grandmother. She too resides in the Orlando, Florida area, where she first applied her talents in children's program development at the Disney Institute. Her background includes creative ideation consulting and consumer market research for Fortune 500 companies. Additionally, she freelances as an editor and writer, and can be contacted at www. wordofmouthediting.com. Michelle treasures the time she spends with family, and hopes to someday become half as good a grandmother as her own mother.

CPSIA information can be obtained at www.ICGtesting.com
Printed in the USA
BVOW04s2335201213

339733BV00009B/65/P